AMEN *and* GOOD MORNING, GOD

AMEN

and

GOOD MORNING

GOD

A BOOK OF
MORNING PRAYERS

BY
JO HUDDLESTON

Tyndale House Publishers, Inc.
Wheaton, Illinois

Library of Congress Cataloging-in-Publication Data

Huddleston, Jo,   date
   Amen and good morning, God : a book of morning prayers / by
Jo Huddleston.
      p.   cm.
   ISBN 0-8423-1667-1 (pbk.)
   1. Prayers.   2. Christian life.   I. Title.
BV245.H76   1995
242'.8—dc20   95-33085

Printed in the United States of America

01   00   99   98   97   96   95
 7   6   5   4   3   2   1

Do not be anxious about anything, but in everything, by prayer and petition, with thanksgiving, present your requests to God. And the peace of God, which transcends all understanding, will guard your hearts and your minds in Christ Jesus.

Philippians 4:6-7

CONTENTS

Introduction . . . . *xi*

Aging *1*

Anger *3*

Brokenness *4*

Children *6*

Commitment *10*

Control *11*

Depression *13*

Discontent *14*

Discouragement *16*

Dishonesty *18*

Doubts *22*

Faithfulness *23*

Fatigue *27*

Forgetfulness *29*

Forgiveness *32*

Friendship *35*

Giving *36*

Gossip *39*

Gratitude *42*

Greed *46*

Grief *48*

Hate *49*

Health *50*

Idolatry *53*

Independence. *56*

Interference *59*

Jealousy. *61*

Maturity. *63*

Obedience *66*

Parenting *68*

Pessimism. *69*

Pride. *72*

Priorities *74*

Quarrels. *76*

Regret *78*

Resentment *81*

Revenge *84*

Secrets *86*

Self-Esteem *89*

Separation *93*

Sorrow *96*

Standing Firm *98*

Stress *100*

Stubbornness. *103*

Suspicion *106*

Temptation. *109*

Unbelief *110*
Unmet Expectations *112*
Weaknesses *114*
Worldliness *117*

INTRODUCTION

Many days I grope for a lifeline of escape from the swelling waters of heartache and frustration. Some mornings I'm almost overcome by obstacles that reach from all sides, seeking to trip me up. To prepare for each new day, I share the fears and longings of my heart with God, telling him exactly how I feel. Morning prayer allows me to climb onto God's lap and find support to help me through the most ordinary day or through the funeral; to help cope with a toddler's tantrum or an adolescent's rebellion; to help mend bruised relationships. By focusing on God's promises, I guard against limiting his power. When I team with God to begin each morning, laying my weaknesses before him, I can meet my problems with divine strength. Whether the day presents valleys or mountaintops, God is our able guide. He awaits our invitation to walk with us daily. As you read these pages, may they help you know each morning that

> *The Lord is close to the brokenhearted*
> *and saves those who are crushed in spirit.*
> *A righteous man may have many troubles,*
> *but the Lord delivers him from them all.* (Psalm 34:18-19)

AGING

God,

My odometer just clicked over to another zero! Oh my, these birthdays with zeroes on the end certainly are gaining ground on me. For just a few minutes this morning as I looked in the mirror, I searched for new wrinkles. Then I made myself a promise: Whenever I think about the years piling up, I'm going to count the blessings each of my years has brought me, instead of counting wrinkles. If you hadn't given me every year of my life, Lord, just think of the good things I'd have missed! Thank you for being the giver of blessings.

AMEN *and* GOOD MORNING, GOD

God,
I can see the fear and uncertainty in my parents' eyes.
They've become so fragile. So vulnerable. Where have
the years gone? When did I become the parent and
they the children? They've phoned already this morning for me to come over. I want to help my parents in
their need, but, Lord, my plate is already full. I've got a
family and children of my own to watch out for. How
can I stretch myself in several directions at the same
time? I'll need all twenty-four hours to do what needs
doing for everybody! And what will that leave for me?
Nothing. Oh, listen to me! Please, God, don't turn
away from my whining. Help me to recall those years
when my parents took loving care of me. Now, when
they can't adequately care for themselves or each other,
I'll do my best to fill the role of parent to my parents.
When they need physical care and emotional support
I'll try to be that for them. Thank you for walking with
me today.

AMEN *and* GOOD MORNING, GOD

ANGER

God,

I almost lost it just now! Can you believe it, a wrong number at five o'clock in the morning! The baby's not even up yet! I don't hear her, so maybe the call didn't wake her and she'll sleep a while longer. People should watch what they're doing when they're using the telephone. They have no consideration for anybody else, calling at this hour of the morning! Oh my, listen to me. I've done the very same thing myself. Well, not before daylight, but I have punched the wrong numbers. Lord, please forgive me for my rudeness just now on the phone. We all blunder now and then. But you know that better than I, don't you? Please help me to be more understanding of others' mistakes, recognizing my own as well. Perhaps you engineered that call, Lord. As I lie here, the only one awake in the house, the quiet brushes across my sleepy eyes like a soothing spring breeze. Thank you for these private moments with you before the busyness of the day begins.

A M E N *and* G O O D   M O R N I N G ,   G O D

BROKENNESS

God,

Do you really keep your promises? I can't go any farther on my own, so today I'm taking you at your word. I need a large measure of that divine strength you offer so many times. Strength to hold me up and get me past my desperation. Thank you for your grace on my behalf.

BROKENNESS

God,

I can't find you this morning. Help me, Lord! Only your strength can break through this feeling of hopelessness. Help me to find warmth in your wondrous sunshine, comfort in the rebirth of springtime. I'm staggering from the blows of one disappointment after another. Please shower me with your mercy. Thank you for reaching into my disjointed world to pull me through the quagmire of my difficulties.

CHILDREN

God,

I saw the defiance in his eyes this morning. I recall when he took his first steps, pulling against the helping hand I offered. Now as he bursts into his teenage years, family traditions pale in his quest for independence. I watch him rush to become a free spirit, straining against every restriction. He considers any advice to be interference. God, you remember when I sped through this same crossroad, don't you? Thank you for helping me shed the garments of youthful judgments and covering me with the warmth of your protection. Help this young one, too, as he slogs through the winding roads on his way to maturity. Keep him safe today.

AMEN *and* GOOD MORNING, GOD

CHILDREN

God,

You must get tired of my coming to you over and over with the same plea: Please protect them! They're so precious—and so innocent. These little toddlers are apt to waddle into potential dangers. They need your angels hovering over them for their physical safety. God, please shield them again this day from bodily harm and pain. Let your angels stand between them and anything or anybody that would hurt them. I trust you to provide for their safekeeping. And then another area of protection I ask for these little ones: May armies of your angels guard against Satan's attacks as these children grow up and move out into the world. Thank you, God, for loving my children.

AMEN *and* GOOD MORNING, GOD

CHILDREN

God,

I'm sure going to need your help today. Last night I went to bed mad, and this morning I got up still mad. Please forgive me for not resolving my anger. I'm thankful you gave me all my children, but, I declare, this teenager of mine can drive me up the wall! She's gone on to school now, and I'm so sorry I didn't apologize to her. We argued over such a little thing, really. You know all about it. Why do I continue to challenge her over such trifling things? So what if she wants to wear purple every day or sing at the breakfast table? Please, God, help me to reserve my correction for truly significant things. Things that will make a difference in the long run. Please guide my thoughts today and help me to greet my child this afternoon with open, loving arms, overlooking the little things. Help me to be strong enough to say I'm sorry. I praise you for your strength in my weakness.

AMEN *and* GOOD MORNING, GOD

CHILDREN

God,

Today I'm so discouraged. You know I don't want my children left in someone else's care every day. But in these hard economic times, we both must bring home a paycheck just to meet all the bills. I praise you for not letting me face these difficult times alone. Thank you for your faithfulness, Lord, in seeing me through this despairing time in my life.

COMMITMENT

God,

I don't know what today has in store for me. I may face some pain that will crush me, splintering my faith. I may be slapped in the face by a surprising disappointment, or some discord for which no peace appears available, or a betrayal that will break my confidence. But whatever disruptions cross my path today, please remind me that I won't have to meet them by myself. Help me to resist any inclination not to trust in you or accept your help. Please remove all my uncertainty. As I approach the unknown today, I'll rely on your promises to see me safely through. I believe nothing in my life is too big for you to handle. Thank you for giving me just the right amount of your strength today.

AMEN *and* GOOD MORNING, GOD

CONTROL

God,

I can't get a firm grip on anything anymore. I'm losing control of every situation. Everything's falling apart. I feel like I'm inside a kaleidoscope and every turn I make fragments me, disconnects me from reality. When I think I've got all my ducks in a row, I soon find myself unable to govern their direction. You already gave me good advice for my predicament, didn't you? You asked me to be still and recognize that you are God. Sounds simple enough, but I'm too prone to forge ahead without first consulting you. As this day progresses, please continue to remind me that within your control I'll be safer. Today, may I be content to follow your directions, not those of my own making. Thank you, God, for waiting when I tend to strain against your best plans for me.

AMEN *and* GOOD MORNING, GOD

God,

I don't understand why Hollywood hasn't called yet! I'd be one of their best directors out there. I'm always telling everyone what to do! Why am I like this, Lord? After I storm in and take over, I realize my abruptness has offended people. Then I'm forever apologizing. But I'm addicted to being in control. I've tried to stop, but I can't. Please help me to lighten up a little and admit that other people could be as capable as I think I am. Or, at least, if I charge in again today, help me to be gentler and less offensive. Thank you for molding me into what you want me to become.

DEPRESSION

God,

I've come to the end of everything. I don't know what to do. What can I do, Lord? It took all my energy just to get out of bed! I can't break through this strong web of sadness that imprisons me. I need hope. Hope to go on. Hope to get up and get dressed. Hope that will motivate me to get back in there and try again! Please anchor me against today's surging trials. Thank you for encouraging me through your healing hope.

DISCONTENT

God,

I'm so dissatisfied. I'm always reaching for something else: things I don't have, things I can't have. The new car, better clothes, bigger house—they're out of my reach. Like trying to hold the wind in my fist. I know this problem lies within me, Lord. I grumble too much. But I can't change my attitude without your help. And I do want to change. I want to be content to trust in your provisions. Help me to have an uncomplaining acceptance of my life. Remind me daily that only your ways offer lasting contentment. Thank you for giving me your peace today in the middle of my restlessness.

DISCONTENT

God,

Where's my identity as a person? Everybody takes me for granted. I feel Satan's undertow tugging at my ankles. I've lost my focus. Well, I haven't really *lost* my focus; I guess I'm just ignoring it. Maybe that's why each day no longer holds excitement for me, why I'm so bored. Please redirect my concentration today toward you. Thank you for understanding my discontent.

DISCOURAGEMENT

God,

I'm just not going to stand for it! I'm tired of all the injustices of life. It's just not fair! Looks like things won't *ever* go any better for me. I can't swim upstream any longer. I've tried and tried, but I can't keep it up. Not anymore! What am I going to do about it, you say? Well . . . I don't know! Just give up, I guess. But you wouldn't be very pleased with me if I gave up, would you? OK, I'll keep trying, Lord. But every now and then, please give me some reason to hope. I know, I know, you already did that. In your Word. You've never broken a promise. Guess you won't start breaking them now. Please hold me tight, God. I need to feel your comforting nearness today. Thank you for putting up with my complaining one more day.

A M E N *a n d* G O O D   M O R N I N G ,   G O D

DISCOURAGEMENT

God,

If I went to the store and never came back, would I be missed? I don't think so. Oh, some of the things I normally do would go undone. For a while. Until my replacement came on board. Lord, I've never felt so ignored in my life! It's as if I'm a vapor, not needing a kind word or a comforting touch. Nobody pays any attention to me or my needs anymore. They must think I just exist, never needing respect or encouragement. God, I do love them. Please keep me from walking out. Help me to understand their limitations when I feel they've let me down. I'll trust you today to help me to feel a little more appreciated. Then maybe I can get through the day a bit less discouraged. What would I do without you? Thank you for being there when all others disappoint me.

AMEN *and* GOOD MORNING, GOD

DISHONESTY

God,

I guess I was dishonest yesterday. Oh, I didn't set out to tell a lie. I know better than to do that. But I also know better than to do what I did. I acted in a deceitful manner. I stood right there and let them heap credit on me when I didn't earn all that recognition by myself. But, Lord, the others who helped me weren't there. And it was too easy to let the sweet perfume of praise fill my nostrils. Working on that committee had been difficult, time consuming. We did a good job and deserved some credit. But I shouldn't have soaked it all up for myself. I'll go back today and correct the matter. Please forgive me for such willful twisting of the truth. Thank you for renewing my integrity today.

DISHONESTY

God,

Please share your strength with me today as I confront my friend. She told a lie about me. It hurts! I'm not sure which hurts more—what she said or the fact that she would say it. I've cried myself dry over this. People who really know me realize she's spreading untruths. But some people who know little about me will hear this, too, Lord, and they might believe what they hear. Please go with me as I try to convince her to correct this lie. Help me to approach her with loving forgiveness for her unfairness to me. I'll need your help to hold my head up in light of the scandal she's started. I'll have to face people's questioning stares for a long while. Oh, how this one little lie has eaten away at my reputation! Thank you for those who will support me through this.

AMEN *and* GOOD MORNING, GOD

God,

The Yellow Pages should have a listing for "Honest Repairmen." Where do I look? Trying to find a dependable worker these days is like throwing darts at a board with no bull's-eye. Has responsibility gone out of style? Does nobody give honest effort for their pay anymore? I feel cheated when the car breaks down again in a week or the drain clogs up again by nightfall. I don't deal too well with people I can't trust. But I'm going to try again today. Thank you for giving me patience while I look for that honest repairman.

DISHONESTY

God,

I think it's called *pretense*. I pretended to be what I'm not just so I would fit in with the group. Like a little chameleon, I changed to blend in with my surroundings. And so last night, for a short while, I became one of them. But this morning I'm not pleased that I so easily changed myself. Lord, you don't approve of hypocrisy, do you? Please forgive me for being caught up without conscience, leading others to think falsely of me. I should have been more concerned about my relationship with you than with the crowd. Thank you for your forgiveness and for still loving me.

AMEN *and* GOOD MORNING, GOD

DOUBTS

God,

How can I believe in you this morning when everything I've worked for is crashing down around me? It seems the harder I try to follow you, the more setbacks I encounter. Nobody else seems to care whether they please you, and they do fine. Better than I do. I know they are not the ideal I should follow—you are. But, God, it's so difficult! Why can't it be easier? Instead of this apparent punishment, please reward my honest efforts to do good. Just a little encouragement would do wonders to increase my faith in you. You know I'll always love you, but sometimes your way gets a little slippery with my tears of disappointment. Forgive me for wanting to give up so often. Thank you for helping my faith grow stronger for the tough times.

A M E N *and* G O O D   M O R N I N G ,   G O D

FAITHFULNESS

God,

I'm not very successful if I follow you halfheartedly. If I don't put complete trust in you, then my faith weakens. I understand your jealousy when I traipse around from one attraction to the other. My goal is to please you, Lord. Thank you for keeping me strong today. Strong enough to concentrate on you as my leader, not scattering my trust among less important things.

FAITHFULNESS

God,

You've never failed me! Everything you've promised, you've provided. How faithful you are to do what you say you'll do. Your eternal faithfulness sometimes causes me to wonder at how often I must disappoint you. I do my best to please you, coming up well short of what you probably expect of me. Lord, help me today not to give up trying to please you. Thank you for loving me anyway.

FAITHFULNESS

God,

I feel sad hearing about all the turmoil and heartbreak in the world. From this morning's early newscast through the late-night wrap-up, I'll hear about the plight of people around the world. Please restore my faith in you. Empires have been founded on a belief in you, only to crumble when the people deserted those beliefs. The world has gaping wounds that need healing. In your Word you give us the formula for the healing of a land: People only have to turn from their unbelief and accept you. You promise that if people will follow your ways you will love them and bless them. But the warning is clear—don't forget you. Thank you for showing me the way to return to you.

AMEN *and* GOOD MORNING, GOD

FAITHFULNESS

God,

I want to please you every day! Give me strength today to resist all temptations to deny you. With your protection, my loyalty to you will not weaken. Thank you for helping me resist anything that would dilute my love for you. I don't ever want to be swayed by others to look elsewhere for happiness. Let me be an example to those around me—an example of loving faithfulness to you. May I always show complete trust in you without doubting or questioning your involvement in my life. Thank you for the joy of living for you.

FATIGUE

God,

I'm drained of all energy this morning, unable to tackle all that I must do today. Thank you for your promise of rest when there's not enough of me to get everything done. Please, Lord, remind me to accept your gift of rest before I begin each new day.

FATIGUE

God,

I keep coming back to you for help. I'm fatigued to the point of giving up. My mind is completely unwound. So much is buzzing around in my head, I can't think straight. I'm so tired that I can't make my body do what I want it to do. I have so much to do today. I've got to get up and get going. Right now! But my body is not willing to go a step farther. Lord, did you cause this exhaustion so I'd change my pace? Well, if so, it worked. Thank you, Lord, for giving me time to reflect on you — on your strength that awaits me if I'll only ask for it. Thank you for your presence even when I'm too busy to remember you.

AMEN *and* GOOD MORNING, GOD

FORGETFULNESS

God,

I get into so big a hurry. I ran on ahead of you this morning. I just rushed out on my own schedule, not once thinking of you. I had complete confidence in my own ability, doubting you could help me. But when my plans met defeat after defeat, I began to wonder why. Now I call on you to please stay with me the remainder of the day. Thank you for using the early morning's setbacks to teach me a lesson. I won't doubt the value of your presence in whatever I do.

AMEN *and* GOOD MORNING, GOD

FORGETFULNESS

God,

I finally did it! I never thought I would become that forgetful. But it happened this morning. I went back into the house to get the dry cleaning and then couldn't remember what I'd gone inside for. I stood there in the kitchen, lost in blankness. I walked through all the rooms, but nothing triggered my memory. I retraced my steps to the car and sat down. Just waiting, like a marooned ship. Then it hit me—the dry cleaning! I muttered the words *dry cleaning* all the way to the closet so my memory gauge wouldn't hit empty again. Thank you, Lord, for allowing me to see the humor in this weakness of mine. Please help me to keep my mind on my business today.

FORGETFULNESS

God,

I feel so helpless when I can't remember someone's name. It's happening more and more these days. I see someone I'm certain I should know, but I can't connect the face with a name. It's doubly uncomfortable when that person remembers *my* name. All I can do is smile. What's wrong with me, Lord? I used to be better at this. Please continue to encourage me as this may happen again today. Thank you for those around me who are understanding of this failing of mine.

AMEN *and* GOOD MORNING, GOD

FORGIVENESS

God,

I guess I'm just the champion of mistakes. I praise you this morning for your forgiving grace. Thank you for the assurance that I can lay my mistakes before you and with loving-kindness you forgive them all. As hard as I try not to, I will sin against you again. But I'm glad I can come to you with my apologies, knowing you'll accept them, and me.

God,

Oh, how I need forgiveness from those around me.
Yesterday as I sought to have my own way, I gave little
thought to the feelings of others. I still can see the hurt
on my child's face and hear the silence of my mate
when I lashed out at them. They couldn't understand
my bad mood. They weren't prepared for my outbursts.
Please help me, Lord, to go to each of them today and
ask for their forgiveness of me and my selfish attitude. I
so want to make it right with them once again. Thank
you for giving me strength today to behave in a more
Christlike manner.

AMEN *and* GOOD MORNING, GOD

FORGIVENESS

God,

Clearing the air between us this morning lifted a burden we both found too heavy. It was as if an artist's brush swept across the lines on our worried faces, relaxing them into smiles. I could feel my joy replenished. Thank you, Lord, for the cleansing gift of forgiveness. Please help me to remember it's a gift that's just as important to give as it is to receive.

FRIENDSHIP

God,

I'm so looking forward to my friend's arrival this afternoon. It's been quite a long time between visits. I'm excited. Will she look the same? Will I? Sometimes long-distance friendships leave a lot to be desired. But this one has lasted through many ups and downs—our families who wouldn't welcome one another, even our pets that fought. Our alliance was destined to survive. Over the years when we couldn't be together, phone calls and letters brought us through personal storms. She's always been there when I needed her. Thank you, Lord, for this true friend. Please help us move right back into step with each other as if we'd never been apart. May we never disappoint each other.

AMEN *and* GOOD MORNING, GOD

GIVING

God,

You are so giving to me! Why, you gave me my very life. I can never repay you; that's not why you're so generous with me, I know. But today, perhaps I can follow your pattern. I may not have a lot of money to give, but I can give of myself as you do. I can give understanding to someone who needs it. To someone in sorrow today, I can offer sympathy. And to anyone who needs encouragement, I can offer them that. You are so quick to give me all these things anytime I ask you. Please put someone in my life today who I can help by being more like you. Thank you for a giving spirit.

GIVING

God,

Do they think I have more hours in the day than they do? Well, I don't! I just wish they'd stop calling on me to do this and do that. I can't get anything accomplished for myself anymore because I'm so tied up with what everybody else thinks I should do. Why can't they find someone else? I have better things I could be doing today besides running around for them! Why me? . . . Oh, Lord, I believe I heard you chuckle just now. What's so funny? What do I have better to do than help others, you say? Well . . . I know others are important. . . . Yes, I did forget for a few minutes there, didn't I? You did give your only Child for the selfish person that I am. Thank you for reminding me to put everything in the right perspective.

AMEN *and* GOOD MORNING, GOD

GIVING

God,

I just can't outgive you! It seems the more I try to give to please others, the more blessings I receive. But you promised me that in your Word, didn't you? You promised that if I give I will receive overflowing returns. Thank you for helping me continue my giving attitude so that I can become more like you today.

GOSSIP

God,

It was so unkind of me. As soon as I did it, I realized what harm I might be causing. Yesterday I passed on the story just like it was told to me, spreading idle words as the truth. I'm disappointed in myself because I didn't resist the temptation to tell the first person I saw. I suppose that person will also turn around and tell somebody else. Please forgive me for being so eager to repeat what I heard without first checking it out. And, anyway, even if it was the truth, I had no business spreading news that might cause someone pain. Please help me to turn away today if I feel an urge to be a talebearer.

God,

Today may you find me as you want me to be. Give me strength to refuse to share in the whisperings of the latest gossip going around. It worms its way into every conversation and commands the attention of all gatherings. Today I'll try to rise above such idle rumors. Thank you for the good sense to say nothing if I can't say something good.

GOSSIP

God,

It seemed like such a tiny thing, really. Until I saw the pain in his eyes and knew I'd somehow hurt him. I didn't realize what I was doing until he poked an elbow in my ribs and gave me that withering look. I stopped in mid-sentence and limped through the rest of the conversation. Maybe the others didn't notice. Please give me wisdom to know when to keep quiet. When he expresses his opinions to me, when he tells me things that happened during his day, help me to consider them as important as he does. Help me to know that when he shares his thoughts with me, he's placing his trust in me — trust that I will guard his feelings and share them with no one else. Thank you that my child feels free to come to me with anything.

A M E N *and* G O O D   M O R N I N G ,   G O D

God,

I'm so glad this morning that I'm acceptable in your eyes. I'm grateful that you don't base your approval of me on external appearance, but on what's in my heart. Sometimes my behavior seems almost to mock what pleases you. But your light of blessings continues to shine on me. You pull me up and point me again toward improvement. Your grace has pulled me through many times when I've almost given up, convinced that nobody cared. Thank you for always receiving me willingly, regardless of my blemishes. No matter how many times I've strayed, your welcome mat is always out when I return.

AMEN *and* GOOD MORNING, GOD

GRATITUDE

God,

I feel so unworthy this morning! I have much to thank you for, but I've neglected telling you. Yesterday I got so busy I didn't talk to you all day. I wouldn't blame you if you turned your back on me this morning. Today I'm not coming with my usual bagful of requests, but instead with a heart full of gratitude. I owe you an immeasurable debt. And sometimes I go for days without even acknowledging you, much less telling you how grateful I am. Thank you for the assurance I feel that even when I'm neglectful of you, you will not forget me.

AMEN *and* GOOD MORNING, GOD

GRATITUDE

God,

Thank you for being there for me whenever I need you. I couldn't get through my days all alone. Knowing you are just a thought away is a comfort I don't ever want to take for granted. You're wonderful to assure me of your help in all situations. I praise you this morning for being my loving Friend.

GRATITUDE

God,

I feel so let down this morning. What do they think? That dirty clothes hampers empty themselves and the clothes skip onto hangers again, clean and ironed? That meals fly from the grocery store and settle on the kitchen table, ready to eat? That the car fills itself up with gas before it's time to go? How do they think all that gets done? I can't help wanting to be appreciated for what I do around here. But, Lord, please give me a love for my family that is not so self-centered. Help me not to keep a record of the times no one seems glad that I'm here. Thank you for helping me love them even when their behavior displeases me. Just like you love me.

AMEN *and* GOOD MORNING, GOD

GREED

God,

Please go with me to the mall today while I'm shopping with friends. I'll need you close by all day because I'll want more than I need. My friends buy without looking at price tags. What a luxury that must be! I guess I'll never know the feeling. I struggle from week to week, just barely making ends meet, hardly ever treating myself to extras. Please help me to remember your promise to meet my needs. Thank you for strength today not to give in to my greedy desires and envious longings.

GREED

God,

I was too eager yesterday to spend my money before I had it. That little plastic card slipped so easily from my wallet. I handed it to the clerk before I knew what I was doing. Buying on credit is convenient—but, oh, it adds up so quickly. And paying what I owe is so difficult! But then Satan makes all his temptations so very attractive and easy for me to fall into. If I cut up the credit card, then I won't have it for emergencies. I just need your help, Lord, to keep me from buying things on credit that I really don't need. Please forgive me for charging so foolishly. Thank you for guiding me today in my efforts to improve my spending habits.

AMEN *and* GOOD MORNING, GOD

GRIEF

God,

Please release me from grief's prison. I need the light of your grace to guide me from this dark tunnel. There can be no explanation. I won't even ask for one. I will lean on your strength again today in my weakness. Lord, please, you've got to make today better than yesterday. Life must get better, or I'll become totally subdued. I feel disconnected and without purpose, robbed of my loved one's presence in my life. Thank you for your promise of eternal peace into which I released her weeks ago. Help me to continue my life in your will until you reunite us in your glorious presence.

AMEN *and* GOOD MORNING, GOD

HATE

God,

I almost packed up and left this morning. How can I love somebody if I don't like him? I hate how he's treated me, but I'm committed to this relationship. Committed to making it work. But, Lord, I don't *like* him! I don't like the way he does some things. I don't know why he can't just change to please me. It would be a simple thing for him to change some of his habits. What? Look at my own behavior, you say? I'm not doing anything wrong—just trying to keep peace around here. Well, maybe sometimes I don't try so hard when I'm complaining. What? Oh, Lord, that won't be easy for me. I never planned to change *myself*. Just some adjustments in *him* would have done the trick. I'll need your help to compromise on the rough spots. And then you'll have to help me to overlook the parts I don't like. Thank you for second chances on relationships.

AMEN *and* GOOD MORNING, GOD

HEALTH

God,

Even this rainy morning doesn't dampen my spirits. When I feel this good, nothing can sour my mood. I cherish the blessings of good health, Lord, and give you all the credit for my well-being today. Even my attitude is much better now that I don't hurt. I'm stronger, ready to tackle whatever you want me to do. Thank you for using dedicated medical people to improve my condition. I praise you for making me well again.

HEALTH

God,

I woke up this morning knowing I'd have to go back to bed. The warning signs crept in from my right side. After just a few steps toward the medicine cabinet, the flashing lights began. Soon I could see only half of whatever I looked at. I'd have to sleep again to regain my sanity. That's the only way I can cope with these awful headaches—my medication and a dark room. They call it migraine, Lord. And it's so devastating! The headache renders me useless for a few hours. There's no way to fight it. I know the headache is more powerful than I am, and so I give in to it. Thank you for watching over me on these bad days as well as my good ones.

A M E N *and* G O O D   M O R N I N G ,   G O D

HEALTH

God,

It's so wonderful to feel good today. You know about all my many parts. Only you can fine-tune them until they perform together like a well-rehearsed orchestra. It's a great day when I feel fit all over. I thank you, Lord, for my victory over pain today. Please forgive me when I go my way, not stopping to thank you for every blessing I enjoy.

IDOLATRY

God,

I think someone I love is putting something ahead of you. But I can't ignore him because of his choices. He needs my love, not my rejection. Help me today to tell him about you. Again. Let your love flow through me as a witness to the joy-filled life available when you occupy first place in our lives. Thank you for giving me your strength today to help guide him back to you.

IDOLATRY

God,

I knew things were spinning too fast last night, pushing me off balance. Without your power, I was helpless to step away. I'd become too attached, directing almost all my devotion in the wrong direction. Things always get messed up when I don't put you first. You'd think I'd have learned that lesson by now. But I continue to have no trouble wandering off your path every now and then. Thank you for helping me keep my attention on you today.

I D O L A T R Y

God,

I do so well for a little while. But I'm just not strong enough to turn my back for very long. I know I shouldn't fill my mind with something like this. It's replacing you in my thoughts. But I just can't help myself! I'm drawn, as if by a huge magnet, until I cross over into impurity. I can't beat the strong pull, Lord. I need your help in this. Your help to change my desires. Please make me strong enough today to turn away from this corruption. Thank you for listening.

INDEPENDENCE

God,

Do you laugh when I make all these ambitious plans? Since you already know the big picture, I can just see you shaking your head in amusement. I even think I heard you say, "Why doesn't she check with me first? My directions could save her a lot of unnecessary frustration." I hear, but I don't listen too well, do I, Lord? I still want to do it my way despite the many times I've stubbed a toe. Please help me today not to be my own leader, but to follow you. Thank you for your patient guidance.

AMEN *and* GOOD MORNING, GOD

INDEPENDENCE

God,

I took things into my own hands, and I failed. I didn't once consider if what I did was your will or whether you'd approve of my methods. Thank you for opening my eyes to the fact that I was like a child, wanting no controls. Wanting to be free of all restrictions. I understand now that I got what I deserved. Everyone gladly left me with all the work after I made sure they knew I could do it by myself. I've got to mend some fences today, Lord. I know now that your plans are much better than mine proved to be. Help me to stay on the same page with you today as I try to correct what I muddled up yesterday. Give me strength to follow you.

AMEN *and* GOOD MORNING, GOD

INDEPENDENCE

God,

Thank you for being patient with me again today. How do you put up with me? It's a wonder you don't just throw up your hands and give up on me. Instead, you continue to bless me with your grace and mercy. When I try to be self-sufficient, you show me I'm not. When I misuse what little authority I have, you remind me that you're my ultimate authority. When I attempt to manage all my affairs without any help from you, you let me know that you alone hold the controls. Thank you for guiding me when I flaunt my independence.

INTERFERENCE

God,

The pain I saw in her eyes doubled inside me. And I caused her that pain! I should have kept my opinion to myself. When will I learn? She's not my little girl any longer. She's all grown up with a family of her own. When I see her about to stumble because of bad judgment or lack of experience, I want to rush to her side — but my help often turns to interference. I think she realizes I mean well. She remains respectful, but at the same time, I hear aggravation in her voice. Thank you for my child. But please help me, Lord, to hold my tongue today and allow her to learn her lessons for herself. Then, if she asks for my help, I'll be close by to give it. After all, that's the way you let me learn so many times, isn't it?

AMEN *and* GOOD MORNING, GOD

INTERFERENCE

God,

According to her, I can't do anything right! I'm so tired of the criticism that I don't know what to do. Can't she see how I hurt when she lets me know, even indirectly, that I don't measure up to her standards? I can't please her. She's never acknowledged any of my accomplishments. She acts like I've never done anything worthwhile all my life. I try, Lord. I really do. I try to be pleasant even in the face of the criticism. But it's so difficult! Whenever I see a glimmer of encouragement, I'm pushed backward by her harsh words. We're just like railroad tracks, never coming completely together in our thinking, our opinions. Close sometimes, but never together. Thank you for enough patience to remain peaceful with her today.

AMEN *and* GOOD MORNING, GOD

JEALOUSY

God,

Why shouldn't I be jealous when I look around at everybody else's life? What happened to all the good things I've been waiting for?! I keep on trying to do right, and where does it get me? I see others whose lives appear so effortless. Whatever they want comes their way at the snap of a finger. I know you have a plan for my life that's supposed to be in my best interests. But sometimes I do wonder about your timing. Sorry, but I do. Forgive me for doubting your judgment. Please help me, Lord, to wait on you and not look for shortcuts today. Give me the desire to stay the course with you. Thank you for continuing to put up with me and my envious ways.

AMEN *and* GOOD MORNING, GOD

God,

It started as a twinge deep inside, then—like water coming to a boil—finally surfaced in my behavior. I finally recognized it for what it was: I was jealous of the woman my son has chosen to love. I thought he was showing favoritism, picking her over me. After all, I'd spent his entire life with him. Now he had directed his attentions toward another woman! At first I was intolerant. He was my possession; I'd raised him into the man he'd become! I thought I had a rival for his love. But I've decided his love for me is unchanged. He's just discovered a new kind of love he can share with her. And she isn't taking him away from me. She's loving him, too. And that's what I want for him—happiness and love with someone he can spend the rest of his life with. Thank you, Lord, for bringing this woman into my son's life and for giving me the good sense not to act hostile toward her today.

A M E N *and* G O O D   M O R N I N G ,   G O D

MATURITY

God,

He's sixteen today. Sixteen going on twenty-five. We're going for the driver's license this morning. Oh, the freedom and independence that little piece of paper will give! I've been there. I also thought myself invincible, beyond harm's way. Thank you for bringing me through those carefree years when I thought only of myself. No thought at all that you watched over me. You did, of course, or I would have self-destructed long ago. Please watch over this new sixteen-year-old as he sometimes soars on foolish wings. As he listens more to his peers than to you and his parents. Please bear with him through his years of impatient recklessness. Situations will come when he needs you and will call out to you. He may not realize your nearness, but please do stay near him, waiting for his call. Thank you for staying close to this child who so naturally longs to become an adult.

AMEN *and* GOOD MORNING, GOD

MATURITY

God,

I screamed at my kids this morning. Several times. Once I hollered, "Act your age!" I got their attention, all right—but only because of my awful attitude. The children *were* acting their age. After all, they're just kids. But I wonder if yelling at them was true to *my* age. I guess I didn't give them a very good model of adult behavior, did I, God? On days like this you probably wonder if I'll ever grow up. I need your help to complete the growth process in my life. Mature me emotionally to match my years. Thank you for being patient with me as I continue to develop. My goal is to become like you. Please forgive my mistakes.

MATURITY

God,

You must have put merry-go-rounds here on earth to give me adventures of imagination. I can lay down all this heavy adult stuff for a few glorious minutes whenever I sit astride a handsome, strutting pony. And then there are the bicycle rides, the yard swings, hide-and-seek games, checkers, ice-cream cones. . . . Thank you for these times when I can forget daily pressures and frustrations. I hope you don't mind my enthusiasm this morning for these wonderful "childish" things in life.

OBEDIENCE

God,

I want to hide from you this morning after what I did last night. I knew I was going against your desires. And even against my better judgment—if I have any better judgment. Sometimes I wonder. I'm sure feeling guilty this morning for disobeying you. And here I come, asking you to forgive me one more time. When will I ever learn to trust you completely instead of following my own impulses? It's never best when I leave you behind. It's like I'm lost in Satan's murky waters, paddling with a feather. Please help me to submit to your guidance today. Thank you for strengthening my heart's commitment to you.

AMEN *and* GOOD MORNING, GOD

OBEDIENCE

God,

I'm content this morning, saturated with your love. This is a familiar feeling when I completely obey you. You know what's best for me. Sometimes it's not easy, Lord, to have faith in what you'll do in my life. Often I roam far from your purposes, choosing my own directions. But so many times the paths I pick soon become choked with the thick underbrush of Satan's temptations. And instead of turning around and returning to your ways, I blunder on ahead, inflicting injury on myself. I never thrive for very long behaving in such a manner. Thank you for the benefits of your loving restraints.

AMEN *and* GOOD MORNING, GOD

PARENTING

God,

Whew! I feel like I just walked across a mile-long minefield! Did I survive? Let me see . . . I believe so. I think everyone got up on the wrong side of the bed this morning. Tempers flared. I must have defused a dozen ticking bombs before I poured the juice. And a dozen more before the school bus came. I may outlive my children because their explosive tempers might lead them to commit—oh, perish the thought! Maybe their friends will distract them from taunting each other now that they've gone to school. Thank you, Lord, for supplying calm during all the tantrums this morning. Please bring the children home this afternoon in a more pleasant mood, all crises reduced to simple sibling rivalry.

AMEN *and* GOOD MORNING, GOD

PESSIMISM

God,

Thank you for changing my mind. I was running low in spirits this morning. You know how badly I wanted to win last night. But even as I face this defeat, your promises give me reason for hope. Maybe you do have something better planned for me. I'll rely on you to help me to hold up until my situation improves. Instead of having such a gloomy outlook on life, I'll try to see good in everything today. Thank you for encouraging me to hope.

PESSIMISM

God,

I feel as effective today as a lamp without a lightbulb. Nothing turns out right for me anymore. Please help me not to dwell on the worst that could happen, but instead to concentrate on all the wonderful blessings that have come my way. I need to feel good about today. Thank you for helping me rid my mind of negative thoughts.

PESSIMISM

God,

Please help me to improve my attitude today. My view of life has become deeply distrustful, my mood disagreeable. Lately I've not included you in my life, Lord, and I've become so depressed. Please reach down and pry me from this suction of gloom I've chosen. If I remain here, I can't enjoy your presence. And without your presence, there's no hope or joy for each day. Thank you for your promise to love me no matter what my mood.

PRIDE

God,

Help me today not to be haughty. I'm no better than any of the others. It just so happens that today I'll be the leader. Nothing more than that. Any one of the group could do the same job, I'm sure. Don't let me fool myself into believing I hold the patent on superiority. That kind of self-deception will lead to my ruin as your ambassador. That kind of arrogant behavior on my part could turn people away from you. Instead, Lord, I want to draw people to follow you. Thank you for your lessons in servanthood. Today if I will only remember how you lived your life, I will sow spiritual joy and not reap spiritual decay.

AMEN *and* GOOD MORNING, GOD

PRIDE

God,

The lust for worldly power turned my head until I hardly recognized myself. I chased after the praise of my peers, forgetting that *your* approval should be my goal. Lord, I followed this path of self-righteousness until I almost became numb to your prodding my conscience. I set myself high on a pedestal of importance, only to fall hard from the lofty heights of excessive self-esteem. Such a conceited attitude was dangerous, opening the doors for other weaknesses to creep into my life—weaknesses that could cause people to question my motives and hinder them from coming to you. Please forgive and remove my ample pride, replacing it with a humble spirit. Thank you for taking your rightful place in my life once again this morning.

AMEN *and* GOOD MORNING, GOD

PRIORITIES

God,

You have first claim on my attentions, but through my haste I've disregarded your importance in my life. In my neglect of you, I've proven myself unresponsive and disrespectful. I've willfully denied you a place in my heart. Please return to my life today, making my thoughts and actions worthy of you. Thank you for forgiving my neglect.

AMEN *and* GOOD MORNING, GOD

PRIORITIES

God,

It seems I'm always doing things I didn't intend to do. And things I should do, I never get done. I try to plan well, but I can't seem to stay on track. I'm just not strong enough to make it work, and I can't fix it, Lord. But you can, if I'll only let you. Thank you for giving me enough faith today to depend on you for solutions.

QUARRELS

God,

Thank you for answering my prayers. Thank you for last night's truce. And such a good place for the reconciliation to happen—at a family reunion! Our clan has returned at last to what it once was: one big happy family. Since Cain and Abel, rifts have torn families apart and shredded emotions. I know our family is no better than any other, but what a blessing to see happy tears of harmony. Thank you for restoring our family and enabling us to mend fences. Please enlighten all families everywhere, and countries as well, to the healing power of your love—the answer to all quarrels.

AMEN *and* GOOD MORNING, GOD

QUARRELS

God,

I was so unfair. I'm ashamed, now that I've had time to think about all I said. Why couldn't I just stop before everything blew up? With all the overtime my husband's putting in, how *could* he do his share around here? But there I went, first thing this morning, jumping all over him. Telling him this needed fixing, that needed doing. When he remained quiet, not saying anything, I thought he was ignoring me. Now I've decided he may have been trying to keep peace between us. Again. I would have been smarter if I'd kept quiet, too. He'll call me later this morning, asking how things are going. He'll promise to get to all the things I nagged him about. And he'll probably even apologize for our argument, the one I started! Thank you, Lord, for my spouse's quiet, loving nature.

A M E N *and* G O O D   M O R N I N G ,   G O D

God,

I can't find an eraser big enough to rub out all my mistakes. I'm so sorry I've made a mess of everything. But now I can't undo the hateful things I've done. I can't bring back any of the words I've spoken in anger. If only I'd treated other people the way I wanted them to treat me! I bolted ahead without you, certain I knew best. Well, it looks like I didn't. I need to start a fresh record. Thank you for the salve of your forgiveness for the sores of my contrite heart. Please help me to turn away from my tangled past and follow your sweet leadership today and in the future.

AMEN *and* GOOD MORNING, GOD

REGRET

God,

Help me as I receive your gift of this new day. Every new day is like flipping to a clean piece of notebook paper, the empty lines waiting to be filled. What I do today will turn the blank lines into another chapter in the story of my life. Please forgive me for yesterday's mistakes. Dwelling on them serves no good purpose, for regret is like cancer, eating away at the good parts. Help me to fill today's clean slate with words and actions pleasing to you. Thank you for another new beginning.

REGRET

God,

Thank you for time's healing massage. Please forgive my lack of belief that when you forgive, you also forget. I've tried to forget, too. But it's really not that easy for me. Because I want to please you so badly, it breaks my heart that I disappointed you those many years ago. I still hurt because I was such a failure. I had one thing to do, and I didn't do it right. And then, instead of trying harder, I just gave up. You've long since forgiven me; I know that. But forgiving myself is another matter. I always wonder what would have happened if I had stayed. Tried again. But had I not moved on, I wouldn't be right here today. I wouldn't be blessed with the joys you've placed in my life since that time. All that surrounds me must surely have been in your plan for me. Please help me to stand within your will each new day of my life.

A M E N *and* G O O D   M O R N I N G ,   G O D

RESENTMENT

God,

Please help me today to keep my irritation from turning into smoldering resentment. Maybe she didn't intend to ignore me, but that's the feeling I got. She's always seemed to have this air about her like she's better than I am. Well, I'm not so sure she is. Maybe she does have designer clothes and a new car, but that doesn't make me any less valuable. Maybe she didn't mean to hurt my feelings. But she did. I need your attitude of grace to deal with this. Thank you for helping me dismiss her snub as unintentional. I hope it was. I'll try to remain friendly even to those who aren't very nice to me and depend on you to heal my hurt feelings.

AMEN *and* GOOD MORNING, GOD

God,

How could these little children know I needed some time alone? They can't sense my adult problems. Nor should I expect them to. All they need to know is that I'm here for them. Whatever time they want with me is theirs just for the asking. I can take care of all those other things later; my chores will wait for me. But my children will grow up and move out all too soon. Right now, Lord, I want to smooth out the rough spots for them like you do so many times for me. Thank you for helping me look wisely at their latest interruption, not considering it an invasion of my privacy. Help me today never to resent any time I spend with my children.

AMEN *and* GOOD MORNING, GOD

RESENTMENT

God,

I follow all the rules. I put you first and tithe to the church. I try not to speak ill of anyone. I volunteer when help is needed. I vote and obey speed limits. And where does it get me? Always confined and behind, just like I am today. I see those people around me who don't love you, but they continue to prosper. They never seem short of money or burdened with needs they can't meet. Their whole lives appear to go smoother than mine. Yes, I resent it, Lord! But then you said I'd have moments like this when I'd be tempted. Tempted to throw up my hands and join them. Oh, it would be so easy. Following their lifestyle, I'd have more money and more free time for myself. I wouldn't be bound by a lot of responsibilities. I could even sleep late on Sunday mornings! But then, I'd be giving you no glory if I lived that way. And I do want to honor you in everything I do. Help me to keep my eyes on you and on your plan for my life. Thank you for understanding and removing my resentment.

AMEN *and* GOOD MORNING, GOD

REVENGE

God,

I praise you that I don't have to be concerned about getting even with them. Sure, I'd like to see them get a dose of their own medicine. They discarded me like yesterday's garbage. But I'll leave their payback to you. I'm confident you'll take care of the situation exactly as it needs to be handled. Thank you, Lord, that I can release my desire for vengeance, waiting on your will. Help me to shower them with kindness and love instead, so they may see you in me. May everything I do today be pleasing to you.

REVENGE

God,

You'll have to help me today, or I'm sure to jump in with both feet to get back at him! It was so unlike him to join the others in their insensitivity toward my feelings. He knows what I think about such matters, and usually he listens with an open mind. But there was strength in their numbers, all of them ganging up on me and my opinions. And he hasn't even apologized yet! I'm angry at him for all this, and I want to see him get repaid for how he made me feel. I want him to feel the same sting of ridicule that I felt. Please forgive me for my vengeful attitude this morning. Lord, you promised you'd take care of times like these. But it seems you're so slow with your revenge. Can't you hurry up a little bit? In the meantime, thank you for helping me be patient enough to continue loving him with your love.

AMEN *and* GOOD MORNING, GOD

SECRETS

God,

If he knew my secret thoughts this morning, what would he think of me? Would he still love me? Lord, I need help to control my inner emotions. To keep my mind centered on you so I won't give in to such destructive thinking. Please don't let my thoughts pass across my lips. They would be so hurtful to him. Why can't love continue as blind as it begins? Blind to his habits that annoy me and his faults that I never noticed before. I need to do away with these hateful thoughts. With your strength, I can. You know me so well and you still love me. Thank you that your love for me is stronger than I deserve.

AMEN *and* GOOD MORNING, GOD

SECRETS

God,

She shares her little secrets with me, certain that I won't disclose a word to anyone. Please help me today not to do or say anything to damage this bond with my child. Thank you for her trust in me.

SECRETS

God,

Looks like I'd know by now that I can't keep anything hidden from you. Whenever I do something I shouldn't and think I've gotten away with it, the guilt sets in. And I can't go on very long with that guilt burning me like acid. Well, as you know, I did it again. This morning I thought it was such a little thing, what would it matter? But in your plan, there's no such thing as a "little" wrong, is there? I tried coloring in a gray area so I'd be more comfortable. But that's not the way you have it planned. So, once again, I've been foolish to think you wouldn't know. Thank you for forgiving my indiscretions and removing my guilty feelings. Your way is the only way. Please help me to remember that today.

AMEN *and* GOOD MORNING, GOD

SELF-ESTEEM

God,

Peer pressure knows no age boundaries. I so want to belong. Why don't they want me, Lord? It hurts when I'm not accepted. They're so confident, so sure of themselves. And I'm so shy. No wonder I don't fit in with them. I want to be like them, but I'm not. Thank you for continuing to give me your assurance today. Help me to be content with the loyal friends I do have, not yearning for substitutes. Thank you that my circumstances are sufficient.

God,

Today's the big day. I think I'm going to be OK. I'm so grateful you helped me finish the program. I'm a better person for having done so. What a wreck I was when I began here weeks ago. But through your strength I held on, forcing myself each day to face reality. The reality of family and friends depending on me. And what motivation for improvement that is! I feel great. I'm my old self again, dependable, capable. Thank you for instilling self-confidence in me once again. When I receive that certificate of completion today, the award will be going to you as much as to me. Thank you that nothing's too great for you to handle.

AMEN *and* GOOD MORNING, GOD

God,

How could you have put together such an awful piece of humanity? I'll never win any beauty contests! And I'm not coordinated either, Lord. I'm all elbows and big feet. I could never work in a china shop! Why couldn't you have given me more grace? My friends are good-natured about my clumsiness. It doesn't seem to bother them as much as it upsets me that I'm so awkward. Thank you for friends around me. For their love and acceptance. Help me to learn from them how to look past outward appearances and appreciate what's inside a person. Then maybe today I can value myself again. After all, you made me. I must have some worth, or you wouldn't have bothered!

AMEN *and* GOOD MORNING, GOD

SELF-ESTEEM

God,

This morning I no longer feel like I'm walking on a high wire without a net. You're always there when I need you. Thank you, Lord, for building me up. For loving me even when I'm not very lovable. With you as my friend, I'll always be able to find my way through my difficulties. Thank you for your strength that changes my weaknesses into courage.

AMEN *and* GOOD MORNING, GOD

SEPARATION

God,

I'm here and they're someplace else. They're not far away as miles go, but being separated from them is like doing Sunday without church or eating cookies without milk. Their absence leaves the rooms quiet, the songs unsung. This morning I feel all alone, Lord, incomplete. Please fill the empty spaces for me. Help me to tackle today and all I have to do, anticipating when we'll be together again. Let your love enfold me in comfort, keeping me from the temptations that rush in on the lonely. It would be so easy to accept whatever attraction Satan offers or to give in to the depression of loneliness. But instead I'll trust you to keep my loyalties in order, holding to my faith in you for guidance. Thank you for your loving presence in my life. You're always near, helping me carry this burden of separation from those I love. Thank you that I'm never really alone.

A M E N *and* G O O D   M O R N I N G ,   G O D

SEPARATION

God,

I feel like I'm alone in outer space, floundering with nothing in sight to grab onto. Where are you, God? I thought you said nothing could separate me from your love. But I don't feel your love this morning. I feel isolated. Maybe it's my fault. Have I done something to create distance between you and me? Please remove anything standing between us, any word or deed that has displeased you. Thank you for your promise to stay close to me. Give me your strength not to stray from you today.

AMEN *and* GOOD MORNING, GOD

SEPARATION

God,

I'm completely shattered! Please pick me up and put me back together. I tried to remain calm while my folks were here last night. But when they told me they've decided to separate, I felt violated. My parents . . . at their age! If they divorce, what will we do at Christmas? On birthdays? There'll be no more family reunions. Please, Lord, show me what I can do to help them, whatever their final decision. But, first, please bind up my broken heart with the strong glue of your love. Then I'll go today and share your love with my parents. Thank you for providing me with the necessary strength for this situation.

SORROW

God,

I praise you that in my intense sorrow I can still have hope. Hope that comes from trusting you. When the heavy weight of sadness slows my step, I have hope for a better tomorrow. Through my faith in you, I can call out to you in my distress. With your help I can move through difficult days. Thank you for your care of me during my weakest moments today. I'm grateful I don't have to experience sorrow like those who live without your hope.

SORROW

God,

I miss my mother this morning. My real mother. Next time I go to visit her we'll have to get acquainted all over again—if she can understand who I am at all by then. Fingers of the disease run through her mind, plucking away her memories. Where has my real mother gone? Does any bit of her remain, crouched behind those searching eyes? Those eyes that smiled at me and wept with me as I grew up. Now I cry for myself, and she looks on in complete bewilderment. I reach to comfort her, but I need consoling myself. Thank you, Lord, for courage to face the anguish that lies ahead as her condition worsens. Help me through the miserable days of having a mother but not really having one at all.

AMEN *and* GOOD MORNING, GOD

STANDING FIRM

God,

Last evening indecision clouded my convictions like fog. I sat there wondering if I should say anything or remain silent. Why didn't I speak out, Lord? Please forgive my silence. One or two in the group glanced at me, expecting me to say something. Normally I do, even though I'm always outnumbered. But, frankly, last night I was just tired of beating my head against the wall every time the same topic came up for discussion. I didn't sleep much last night, struggling with my lack of reaction yesterday. So I've decided I won't straddle the fence again. I'll state my opinions based on your Word and then stand strong in my belief in you—whether in the privacy of my own home or facing the judgment of a crowd. Please strengthen my trust in you today.

AMEN *and* GOOD MORNING, GOD

STANDING FIRM

God,

I praise you for intervening in my lifestyle. The dead-end street I chose was short, leading nowhere. But, of course, I wouldn't listen to anybody who told me so. Only you could get my attention. Thank you for seeing the good in me and turning me around. I'm whole again. I'm all together now. I've taken control of my choices, making good ones, not being influenced by the "wrong crowd." Please help me to be strong today against almost certain temptations to return to my old way of life. I'll be facing familiar jeers because I've chosen your way. Please grant me your mighty strength in my daily personal battles.

AMEN *and* GOOD MORNING, GOD

STRESS

God,

Magazine covers at the grocery checkout scream messages about how to relieve stress. But I don't have time for their warm, relaxing baths. Even if I could find the time, what would I do with the children? We'd all end up in the bathroom together. All in the smallest room in the house. Now that would really take care of my stress level, wouldn't it? And forget the candlelight dinners the magazines suggest! I just have too much to do, Lord! Why me? Why can't somebody else around here do some of these things? Or, better yet, maybe some of these things don't actually need doing. Maybe that's it. Of course, I have too much to squeeze into a day, but who made the list? I did. Please help me this morning to take a wiser look at what I've allowed to crowd me into a corner. Help me to remember there's time enough to do whatever you have planned for me to do. Thank you for helping me put the hours of my day back into proper perspective.

A M E N *and* G O O D   M O R N I N G ,   G O D

STRESS

God,

I search and search for solutions, looking for anything to lighten my load. I feel the venom of stress as it gradually poisons every part of my life. But I find in your Word that I don't have to be a prisoner of the anxieties of this world. That I can turn them all over to you, and you'll give me strength to meet each day without getting all uptight. You're ready to help whenever I transfer my heavy loads to you. Thank you for providing me an escape from the tensions assaulting me every day. I feel refreshed knowing you will help me with today's cares.

AMEN *and* GOOD MORNING, GOD

STRESS

God,

I was headed right into a buzz saw that would have spit me out in little pieces. I know by now to expect her criticism. But I guess I always hope for something better every time I'm with her. Her words cut like barbed wire, ripping away at my calm. Any attempt at conversation always ends in disagreement about something I've done or am about to do. Trying to defend my position only makes matters worse. In her opinion, I have no defense. But she's always able to prod me into a discussion anyway. Just now I realized I was getting too agitated to think straight. Thank you for restoring my judgment. Please help me today to respect her friendship but at the same time distance myself from her tirades.

A M E N *and* G O O D   M O R N I N G ,   G O D

STUBBORNNESS

God,

I know I'm stubborn. I've known it for a long time. But, Lord, when other people want to change me, first this way and then that, I don't like it. That's when I dig in my heels. I figure my way is as good as the next person's. You'd like for me to be more open minded? Listen to other opinions? Maybe it wouldn't hurt me too much to give in every now and then. Do you think I might have more friends that way? Lord, help me to take a sincere look at every perspective, valuing other people's opinions as highly as I do my own. Thank you for putting up with my obstinate ways today and for helping me improve.

AMEN *and* GOOD MORNING, GOD

STUBBORNNESS

God,

I've never seen anyone so hard to deal with! Whatever I say, he takes an opposite view just to be contrary. And when he sets his mind, *nothing* will sway him. He thinks he's always right. *Always!* Lord, that's what makes it so difficult for me to be around him. There's no compromise in him. It's his way or no way. Period. Sometimes when he upsets me, I try to share my feelings with him. He tells me I shouldn't feel the way I do. But, Lord, I'm free to have my own feelings, don't you think? I feel so intimidated around him. I allow him to dictate my opinion of myself. Please restore my self-worth. Thank you for helping me today to deal with his mulish ways as you would.

AMEN *and* GOOD MORNING, GOD

STUBBORNNESS

God,

I wouldn't listen, in spite of reason. People who loved me tried to help, but I wasn't ready for help. Didn't think I needed any help. I was having too good a time. I filled every day with my own selfish desires, ignoring all your warning signs. I resisted all persuasion to change my lifestyle. Why change when I was having so much fun! But, Lord, today the things that were fun don't make me laugh anymore. Now I can't find an off-ramp on this fast road to good times. I want to renew my life, bring it in line with your purposes. I realize now I can't do it alone. Please forgive me for being so unyielding in my behavior. Thank you for loving me enough to lift me up and hold my hand as I start my way back.

AMEN *and* GOOD MORNING, GOD

SUSPICION

God,

He betrayed me once. How can I be sure he won't do it again? It's so easy for me to be suspicious of him every time he's out of my sight now. Again this morning I had difficulty being sure he's telling me the truth. I know I must believe him if this is ever going to work. But doubts creep in so often, even though I think he's really trying. Lord, increase my trust in him and in his love. I know you will bless our efforts if we continue to please you with our lives. Thank you for helping me blot out the past and strive toward a better future.

God,

I thought I had all the proof I needed for the ugly accusations I made last night. But once I cooled down and let him explain, it all cleared up like rising fog. How petty of me to rant and rave like that with no certainty in what I was thinking! The clues did all point toward the same conclusion: the scent of perfume that wasn't mine, the matchbook cover from a restaurant where I've never been. But I let myself forget that in his professional life he can't pick and choose his business associates just to placate a suspicious mate. Thank you for helping me realize that sometimes things aren't what they so easily appear to be.

AMEN *and* GOOD MORNING, GOD

SUSPICION

God,

I could kick myself this morning. Why did I listen more to what other parents think instead of having complete confidence in my own child? I'm afraid she sensed my suspicion. And I had no reason to mistrust her. She's a good girl, Lord. I don't ever want to give my child the message that she's less important to me than other people. Even when she may disappoint me, please help me to love her unconditionally—the way you love me. Thank you for replacing any doubts with loving trust.

TEMPTATION

God,

I'm so glad you intervened in my life this morning. Thank you for yanking me away from certain heartache. The distraction wrapped itself beautifully in his silken charms and compliments. The telephone call flattered me, and in just a few moments I would have been out the door. But in your way, you spoke to me of the foolishness of the indiscreet invitation I almost accepted. You made me understand the pain I could have brought to myself and my loved ones had I yielded to the temptation. Thank you for your strength in my unthinking weakness. Thank you for helping me say no.

AMEN *and* GOOD MORNING, GOD

UNBELIEF

God,

Thank you for not deserting me when I question your power. Even though I don't challenge you out loud, I show my doubt when I don't follow your ways every day. Simply by not applying your solutions to my problems I open the door for small amounts of unbelief to collect in my life. Then I begin to hurt, like I'm hurting this morning, because I've distanced myself from you. I miss your comfort just as I miss the sun's warmth when clouds block its rays. Like flowers that wilt without rain, my faith falters unless I stand in your truth. I'm glad you show me the greatness of your support. I praise you for reviving my belief through evidence of your love around me.

UNBELIEF

God,

Why have your blessings dried up this morning? It's as if you went on vacation and didn't return. Are you trying to tell me something? What? What have I done? Did I not talk to you enough? Did I fuss at you too much when I didn't get my way? Well, I can't help it, Lord. Life gets rough. And sometimes I have to go off and try my own way. But I always come back, don't I? I guess I have been away for too long this time. I didn't think you were watching. I didn't think you knew where I was or what I was doing. But I guess no part of my life stays hidden from you. It is just so easy to chase after Satan's temptations, enjoying his instant rewards. It's hard to keep strong faith in you, but I'm trying. Please forgive me when I don't, and give me patience to believe. Thank you for allowing me to come back one more time.

AMEN *and* GOOD MORNING, GOD

UNMET EXPECTATIONS

God,

It's happened again—I'm really deflated. Why do I always expect too much of everybody? But I do, inviting heartache when they don't measure up to what I anticipate. Thank you, Lord, that when others don't meet my expectations today, I can wait on you to fulfill all your promises.

UNMET EXPECTATIONS

God,

Please forgive me for fussing at you last night. I became impatient when I couldn't see my prayers getting through to you. When you didn't give me everything I'd looked forward to, I turned my back on you. I'd convinced myself that if you were all-powerful, you could give me whatever I wanted. Whenever I asked. But this morning I'm a little calmer, more rational. I understand better now. You hear my pleas and know my desires, but you react as my heavenly Father. Just like a good parent, you won't give me everything I want. I'll try to trust you to know what's best for me and have faith that you will meet my needs. I'll still place my hope in you today. Thank you for being tolerant with me.

AMEN and GOOD MORNING, GOD

WEAKNESSES

God,

I can't continue fighting these uphill battles. And they all seem uphill, Lord, never leveling off or letting up. Please blanket me with your power, helping me with my struggles. Please remove the doubts and temptations that invade every day. Thank you that I do get through each problem with just the amount of your strength I need at that particular time. With your grace I claim victory for whatever comes my way today.

WEAKNESSES

God,

On my own today I can't be the beacon you'd have me be. I can't be salt of the earth as you instructed me, flavoring the days with your love. No, I'm just weak, Lord. Overcome by sin and discouragement, I'm quite feeble in my resistance to Satan's persuasions. But the strength I receive from you helps me to glorify your name. Thank you for holding me up in my weakness as you promised.

WEAKNESSES

God,

My world is crumbling because it has turned away from you, weakened by Satan's daily rampage. In this world I find no support for survival. The hurts, the gripping pain, the disappointments all rush in daily. Without your help, these heartaches would surely defeat me. Please apply your power and strength to my many weaknesses. Thank you that today I can lean on you for assurance and encouragement.

WORLDLINESS

God,

The microwave oven has spoiled me! How difficult it is this morning, waiting for the pecan pies to bake in the old oven. And, earlier, waiting for cinnamon toast to get bubbly and crisp the old-fashioned way. Just as the microwave gives me almost instant food, the world offers quick satisfaction for my earthly desires. No wonder my head is turned by the instant beauty and effortless success hawked daily in magazines and on television. But nothing's as easy as it sounds — or quite as rewarding. And it's all so temporary, Lord. The fashions I latched onto last season are out of style now, and I'm supposed to go out and buy all new things again. Even my car, which is fairly new, already sports the old look if measured by the world's yardstick. I try to remember that if I seek you first, I won't be counting on these worldly things that will disappoint me with their eventual emptiness. Thank you that your love is not temporary, but forever.

AMEN *and* GOOD MORNING, GOD

WORLDLINESS

God,

I choose to live by your standards. The world will seldom agree with me and will often try to change my mind. But I'll depend on you for strength to reject Satan's false charms. I won't swap the eternal rewards of your promises for anything this world offers. Not for prestige or position. Not for power or material gain. I praise you that I can stand for your values. Thank you that because of your love for me, I don't have to be devoted to this world and its pursuits. Today I can tend to your affairs, trying to avoid being sullied by this world.

WORLDLINESS

God,

Help me to find my way in the darkness of this world. Please shine your light into the recesses of my heart, uncovering my lust for worldly possessions. I've chased after tangible personal gain instead of waiting on your will for my life. I've become tarnished by the immediate concerns of worldly interests instead of being satisfied with your provisions. I want to deny the desires this world taunts me with because their allure draws me away from you. Thank you for strength to concentrate on you, not the distracting things of the world. If I'll include you in my life today, the illusions of this world will dim. I love you, God.

AMEN and GOOD MORNING, GOD

Do you not know? Have you not heard? The Lord is the everlasting God, the Creator of the ends of the earth. He will not grow tired or weary, and his understanding no one can fathom. He gives strength to the weary and increases the power of the weak. Even youths grow tired and weary, and young men stumble and fall; but those who hope in the Lord will renew their strength. They will soar on wings like eagles; they will run and not grow weary, they will walk and not be faint.

Isaiah 40:28-31

To him who is able to keep you from falling and to present you before his glorious presence without fault and with great joy—to the only God our Savior be glory, majesty, power and authority, through Jesus Christ our Lord, before all ages, now and forevermore! Amen.

Jude 1:24-25